Amazing Ants. A Facts and Pictures of Ants

Part of the *Nature Discovery Books for Children Series*

Author: Wild Pages Publishing

Watercolor Illustrations beautifully painted by Maria Apriatova.

Photographs gratefully provided by Hamish G. Robertson, PhD, and Duncan Robertson.

Everyone here at Wild Pages Publishing would like to thank entomologists Nanike Esterhuizen, PhD, and Palesa Natasha Mothapo, PhD. Their help writing, fact-checking, and making suggestions for this book was invaluable. The book is greatly improved because of their contributions! The folks at Wild Pages Publishing are responsible for any mistakes in the book!

Table of Contents

1. Welcome to the World of Ants

Hello, young explorers! Are you excited to learn about some amazing little creatures? Come along as we go on an adventure to discover the fascinating world of ants.

This book is filled with fun facts about the ant's life, its body, behavior, social networks, and much more. But why should you care about ants? Compared to other popular bugs like honey bees, butterflies and ladybugs, ants are often misunderstood and not appreciated.

Sure, ants can be annoying when they join our picnics uninvited or make their little trails around the house... But there's so much more to them than that. They might be small, but ants play a really important role everywhere they live.

Ants really do make the world go round, and you are about to discover how important and interesting these **insects** truly are.

2. To be an Ant

Imagine a world where you are the size of a grain of rice. Everything around you is huge! Every rock, leaf or twig is a major obstacle in your way. Humans are giants who won't hesitate to step on you. Lizards, birds, and other animals are monsters out to get you. Even a drop of rain could drown you!

So, in a world where you seem so small and helpless, how do you survive?

The answer lies in teamwork! Just as there is no I in TEAM, there's also no I in ANT. After millions of years on Earth, ants have become **adapted** to thrive in lots of different places and overcome many different challenges. Everything they do, they do as a team, working together for the greater good of their ant **society**. And with safety in numbers, the big and scary world is not so scary after all!

This ant is lifting a heavy rock over its head! Ants are really strong for their size.

> **Fun fact:** Ants might be small, but they are incredibly strong. Some studies show they can carry up to 100 times their own body weight! If a 10-year-old girl was that strong, she could carry 2 rhinoceroses at the same time!

3. The Queen and Her Colony

Ants are social insects that live and work together in groups called **colonies**. An ant colony has at least one **queen**. Some colonies have hundreds of queens, each with their own nest. Queen ants can live for 30 years! Most queen ants have wings.

When a queen is ready to start her own colony, she flies around searching for male ants. After the queen mates with one or more male ants, her wings fall off. Then she finds a dark, safe place to start a new colony and starts laying eggs.

In some ant colonies, the queen doesn't have wings. She attracts male ants with a special scent that helps the males find her. Males get into the colony and mate with the queen. Then the queen starts laying eggs.

The Ant Life-Cycle

After the queen's eggs hatch, small worm-like babies called **larvae** are born. With enough food and care, the ant larvae grow and turn into **pupae**. In some kinds of ants, the pupae are inside cocoons. Other types of ants don't spin cocoons. With or without a cocoon covering them, the pupae finally become adult ants.

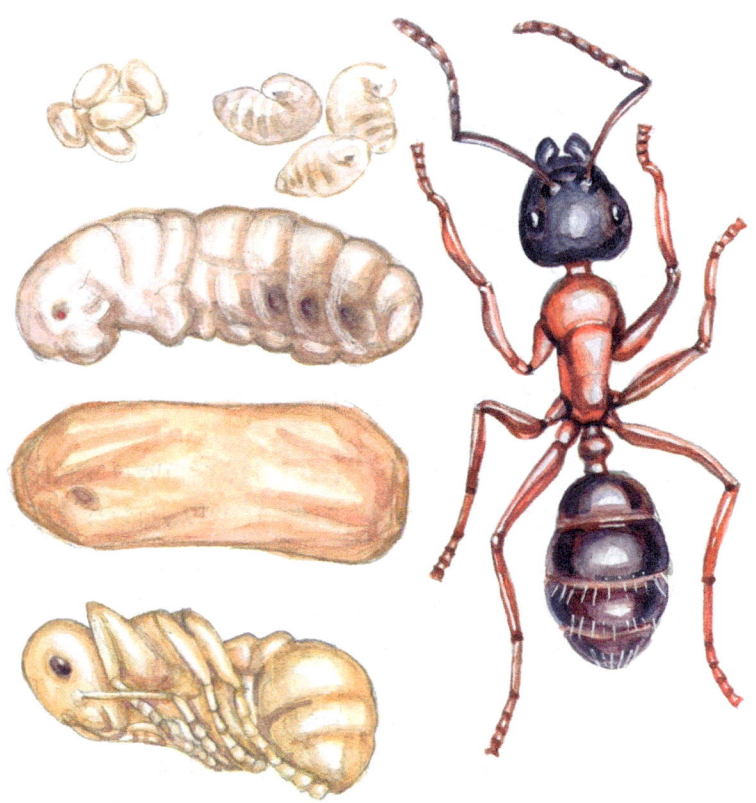

On the left at the top of the illustration are eggs and next to the eggs are tiny larvae. Below that (from the top down) are an older larva, cocoon, and pupa. On the right is an adult ant.

Fun fact: *Have you ever seen the cocoon of a moth? Inside that cocoon is a pupa too! And just like caterpillars turn into adult moths inside their cocoons, ant larvae turn into adult ants inside their cocoons.*

All the Queen's Daughters

Some queens lay thousands of eggs each day. The queen lays both fertilized and unfertilized eggs.

If an egg is fertilized, the ant will be female. These females are the queen's daughters. They are known as **worker ants**. Most of the ants in the colony are workers. Even though worker ants are all female, they can't lay eggs. Only the queen can lay eggs.

All worker ants start their life doing chores inside the nest like building tunnels, cleaning rooms, and looking after other ants. Later in their lives they go outside the nest looking for food. They also defend the colony.

Worker ants can bite their enemies. Some ants can even sting or spray their enemies. But don't worry! Most ants are harmless to humans.

Ants in the same colony are different sizes and have different jobs. (Left to right is a queen, male, and worker)

Soldier Ants

In some ant colonies, there are worker ants called "soldier ants" that are usually bigger than the other ants in the colony. These females have large heads and huge jaws that make them really good at defending the colony. Even though soldier ants guard the colony, they still do all the normal tasks expected of the rest of the female workers.

What About Male Ants?

Did you know that male ants have wings and can fly? They can! For a few weeks every year, the queen lays unfertilized eggs that become male ants. The males leave their homes and fly around looking for a queen to mate with. Sadly, after the male breeds with a queen, he dies.

Fun fact: When it comes to ants, girls rule the world! Female ants make everything work in a colony. Male ants don't do any work. Their only purpose in life is to reproduce with new queens. This means every ant you see on a trail is female!

4. Where Do Ants Live?

Ants make their nests in many different areas or **"habitats"**. A specific location within a habitat is called a **niche**. Different kinds of ants have adapted to live in different niches.

For example, one **species** of ant can make its nest underground. Another kind of ant might make its nest in a tree, under a rock, in a hollow log, or even in the walls of your house. By living in these different niches, many different species of ants can live happily in the same area.

Ants that live underground dig lots of tunnels that connect the rooms or **"chambers"** of their nest. When building tunnels, the worker ants carry grains of sand out of the nest using their jaws! Sometimes you can see a ring of dirt or sand around the entrance to an underground ant nest.

Fun fact: Ants are found on every continent and in almost every country of the world. The only places they don't live are on a few islands and the frozen areas of Antarctica and the Arctic. Those polar regions are too cold for ants to survive.

Here you can see an example of an underground ant nest with chambers and tunnels.

Living in underground chambers keeps the adults, eggs, pupae, and larvae safe from the outside world. Ants also store food in their underground chambers the way people store food in root cellars or pantries.

Some ants, like leaf-cutter ants that you'll learn more about later, need to keep their nests at just the right temperature and **humidity**. Their nests have many entrances and exits so air flows between the rooms in the chambers. This would be like opening windows in different rooms of your house so the air flows from one room to the other.

5. What Do Ants Do?

Have you ever watched a trail of ants in your backyard and wondered, "What are they doing and where are they going?"

Well, the answer is actually quite simple. These ants are looking for food!

Ants eat almost anything! Some natural foods ants love are seeds, fruits, plant sap, dead animals, and **honeydew**. Honeydew is a sweet liquid made by many different bugs. **Aphids** are a common bug that makes honeydew. You'll learn more about aphids in the "Ants as Farmers" chapter later in this book.

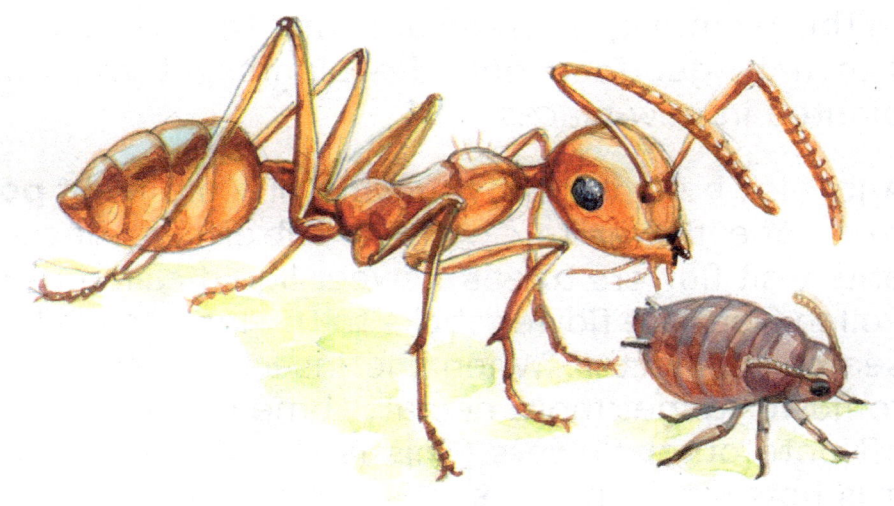

Ants protect aphids from predators and aphids give honeydew to the ants. They help each other.

Partnerships with Plants

Ants help plants in a lot of ways. One way ants help plants is by planting their seeds in new places. That's right, ants plant seeds! Here's how it works...

Some seeds have an extra part on them that ants love to eat. Ants gather these seeds and bring them back to their underground nests. The workers feed the extra part of the seed to their larvae. The uneaten part of the seed is thrown away in an underground chamber. But, even after the ants eat the extra part of the seed, it can still sprout. And sometimes a new plant grows where the ants "planted" the seed in their underground chamber.

In this example, both the ants and the plants benefit. The ants get food and the plants get their seeds planted in new places.

Ants also help plants by moving tiny grains of **pollen** from one flower to another. Butterflies, bees, and ants visit flowers to eat a sweet liquid called **nectar**. Pollen from the flower sticks to the insects while they search for nectar. When the insects go from flower to flower to get more nectar, some of the pollen falls off onto other flowers. This is called pollination and it is how plants make seeds and reproduce.

Insects pollinating plants this way is another example where both organisms benefit. In this case, the plants get pollinated, and the insects get food.

Cleaning the Ecosystem

Besides helping plants, ants also help clean the **ecosystem**. Have you ever wondered what happens to the bodies of dead animals?

Well, dead animals slowly break down into tiny pieces that become part of the soil. This process is called **decomposition**. Ants, flies, beetles, and worms eat dead animals. This is part of the decomposition process, and it helps the nutrients from the dead animals return to the soil.

Fun Fact: Many animals eat ants. In fact, some animals like the Giant Anteater from South America and both the Aardvark and Pangolin from Africa love ants so much that they only eat ants and termites. All these ant-eaters have big claws for digging up ant nests and long, sticky tongues for licking up the yummy ants. Many people eat ants too! You can read more about that in the "Ants and People" chapter later in this book.

Anteaters have long tongues they stick in tunnels so they can eat ants and termites!

6. The Ant Body

Whether you see ants around your house or find them outside in nature, you've probably noticed some interesting things about ants. They have unique bodies and sometimes walk in a line. Let's find out more about ants and their behavior.

What Ants Look Like

How would you describe an ant to someone who's never seen one before? What makes an ant an ant?

Well, ants are **insects**. This means they have six legs just like beetles, butterflies, crickets, flies, wasps, and honey bees.

Like most insects, ants have three main body parts: a head, **thorax** (chest), and **abdomen** (rear end). Most insects also have feelers or **antennae** on their heads.

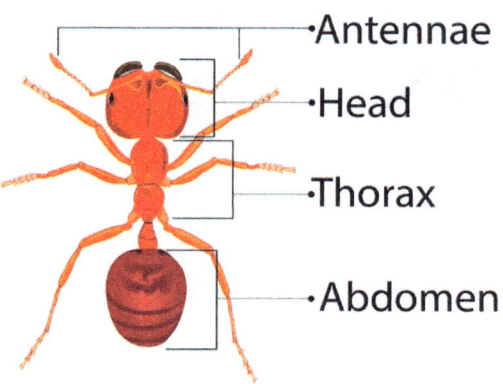

The main parts of an ant's body are its head, thorax, and abdomen. Illustration by Lima Akter.

Have you seen an ant's antennae?

Antennae are super sensitive body parts that sense different chemicals, sort of like our noses. Ants also use their antennae to feel vibrations in the ground.

Although some species of ants have good eyesight, most ants don't see well at all. In fact, some ants are completely blind.

Ants have many of the same behaviors and body parts, but different species of ants look very different from one another. Ants' bodies are sometimes covered in very fine hairs. Some ants have spikes to protect them from **predators** and rival ant colonies!

Ants come in many different colors depending on the species. Ants can be black, yellow, green, red, brown, and almost see-through.

Fun fact: *There are insects that some people call "white ants", but these insects are not ants at all. They are termites! Ants and termites are both insects, but they aren't the same.*

Ants are related to wasps, but termites are in the cockroach family. You can see the difference too. Ants have eyes, and termites don't. Ants have pointed abdomens, and termites have rounded abdomens.

Body size varies a lot between ant species too. Ants can be as small as 0.03 inches or as big as 2.0 inches (0.75 mm to 50 mm) long! You already know that ants in the same colony are also different sizes. The queen is the largest and normal workers are the smallest.

How Ants Communicate

Ants use their antennae to understand the world around them. Their antennae also help ants communicate with each other. All ants make and release odors called **pheromones**. Pheromones are smells used to recognize other ants and share information.

These odors make it easy for ants to identify their family and friends – as well as their enemies. Ants from the same colony smell similar. When ants from the same colony meet each other, they immediately recognize each other's scent and know they are safe.

But ants from different colonies don't have the same odor. If ants from different colonies run into each other, the ants know the other ant could be an enemy because they don't smell the same!

You've probably seen ants going back and forth on the same trail. How do you think the ants know where the trail is?

If you guessed that the ants are following a scent trail, you're right! Ants leave a trail of smelly pheromones for other ants to follow.

See if you can make another guess... What do you think is on each end of the ant trail?

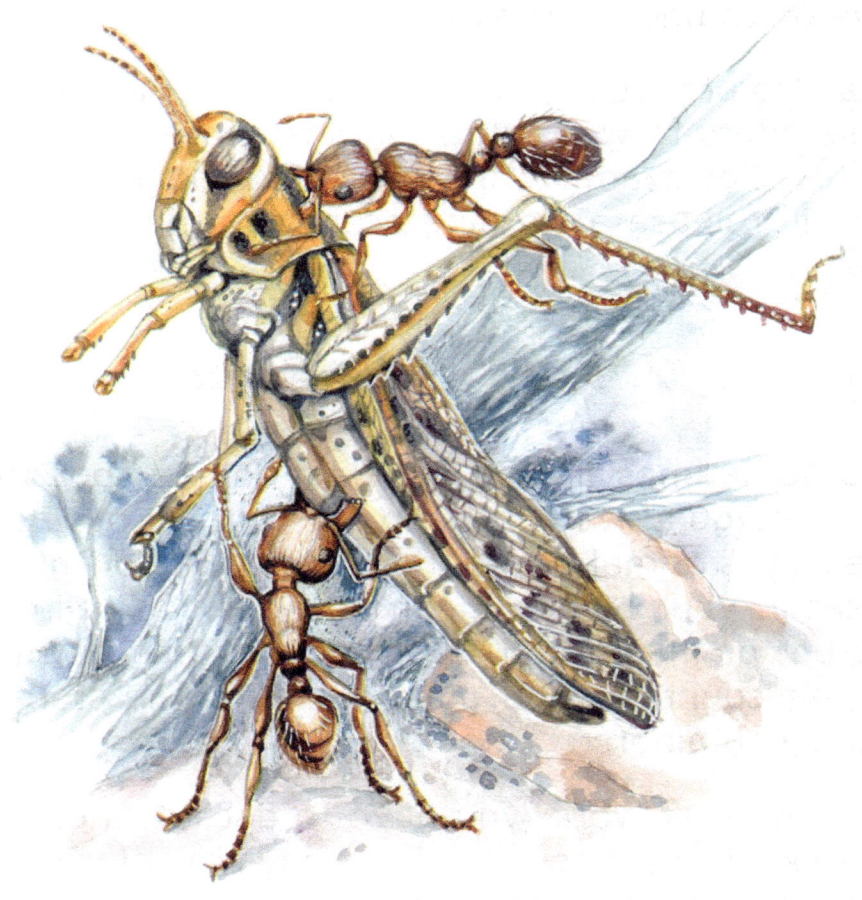

These two ants need help getting this grasshopper back to the nest. They will release an odor that tells other ants there is food on the trail!

If you guessed that there is food at one end of the trail, and the entrance to the colony is at the other end, you are right again!

Ants make new scent trails when they find food. If you want to see ants make a trail, you can put breadcrumbs or something sweet on the ground for them. The ants will make a trail from the treat you gave them back to their nest.

Ants also produce "alarm" pheromones. Ants release these odors to warn other ants that there is danger nearby. For example, if a spider attacks an ant, the ant will release a warning scent so other ants stay away.

7. Ants and People

Ants sometimes invade people's houses, but there are some good ways to keep ants out of your home. One way is to make sure there is nothing for the ants to eat in your house. Clean up after yourself when you eat or make food. Wash your dishes, wipe the kitchen counters, and make sure food is stored in sealed containers.

If this doesn't work, you have to decide whether or not to kill the ant colony. If you have to get rid of the ants, make sure to use **eco-friendly** products.

A relatively safe ant killer is half borax and half powdered sugar mixed together. Sprinkle the poison in places where your family and pets won't find it, but the ants will.

If you decide not to kill the ants, that's great! Ants help people in a lot of ways. As you've already learned, ants are special little creatures with important jobs to do. They pollinate plants, clean up the **environment**, and plant seeds. Ants are important in other ways too.

A lizard is about to eat these ants. Without ants, many reptiles, birds, and other insects would have trouble finding enough food to survive.

Ants help farmers and gardeners keep pests under control by eating the bad bugs that damage food crops. The tunnels ants dig help air get into the soil, and this makes plants grow better.

In some places, people eat ants! In Mexico, ant eggs, larvae, and pupae are made into a snack called *escamoles* or "insect caviar". Insect caviar has a buttery, nutty flavor that most people think tastes delicious.

Fun fact: *Scientists think that the total number of ants on earth could be a mind-blowing 20 quadrillion – that's 20 million billion! This means that there are about 2.5 million ants for every person on earth. That's a lot of ants!*

---

8. Supercolonies

Most colonies don't let ants from other colonies go into their nest. The outsiders might fight with them and steal their food! Even ants that are the same species but from different colonies like to keep to themselves.

However, some species of ants live in peace with other colonies of the same species. They form what is called a "supercolony".

A supercolony is a big group of ants that all recognize each other as family. Ants that form a supercolony can easily outcompete the **native** ants when they move into new areas.

Fun fact: One of the ants you'll learn more about in the "Special Kinds of Ants" chapter is the Argentine ant from South America.

This **invasive** ant species forms supercolonies. They have a massive "megacolony" of ants that all recognize each other as family.

This supercolony stretches across four continents: North America, Europe, Asia, and Australia.

If you took an ant from the Australian colony to the United States, it would be accepted as family in the US colony!

9. Ants as Farmers

Gathering enough food for the colony is a top priority for ants. Most species of ants will eat almost anything they can find: seeds, nectar, bits of human food, and dead animals. Ants are always looking for something to eat.

However, some ants have a great way to make sure they don't run out of food. They farm their own food! Leaf-cutter ants, which you'll read about later in this book, have **fungus** farms.

Many species of ants farm little bugs called "aphids". Aphids are common pests that often damage fruit trees and vegetable plants. Aphids suck the juice out of plants, then they poop out a sugary juice. This sweet liquid is called "**honeydew**", and ants love honeydew! When an ant rubs an aphid's back with its antenna, the aphid releases honeydew.

This Crazy Ant is "farming" aphids to get their sweet honeydew.

The ants and aphids help each other. The aphids help the ants by making sweet honeydew that the ants love to eat. The ants help the aphids by protecting them from predators like ladybugs and wasps. Some species of ants even bring aphids into their underground nests during the winter. The aphids feed on the roots of plants and make honeydew for the ants all winter.

10. Special Kinds of Ants

There are over 15,000 different ants around the world! About 811 species are found in the United States of America. Australia has more species of ants than any other country with over 1,600 different kinds of ants!

We can't talk about all those different ants in this book. We have included some interesting and unique ants for you here though!

Fun fact: Ants have been around much longer than humans – 120 million years, to be exact. That's all the way back to the time of the dinosaurs! Some ants back then were the size of modern-day sparrows! Scientists think there are about 22,000 species of ants in the world today.

Acrobat Ants

Scientific name: *Crematogaster*

- **Number of species:** Around 790 species.
- **Worker size:** Tiny to medium-sized. 5/64"-13/64" (2-5 mm) long.
- **Personality:** Aggressive.
- **What they eat:** Acrobat ants have a general diet, but they eat mostly other insects and sweet foods.
- **Where they live:** All over the world. Most species live in tropical and subtropical areas.
- **Where they nest:** Acrobat ants live above ground, often in trees. Some species live underground.

Acrobat ants drink from a raindrop after a storm.

Acrobat ants get their name because they are flexible like acrobats. They can bend their abdomens, or "tails", backwards up toward their heads. They are also called "cocktail ants" because of the way they angle their tails up like this when they are bothered.

Acrobat ants sometimes bite people if they are scared. They also give off a stinky smell when they are threatened. The smell makes intruders want to go away and warns other ants that there is danger nearby. Acrobat ants can also sting their enemies.

Acrobat ants are fearsome defenders of their nests. If a colony has their nest in a tree, the ants won't let ants from other colonies onto their tree.

This Black Cocktail Ant uses its stinger to defend the colony against invaders.

Argentine Ants

Scientific name: *Linepithema humile*

- **Worker size:** Tiny to small. 5/64"-1/8" (2-3 mm) long.
- **Personality:** Aggressive.
- **What they eat:** Argentine ants eat a lot of different things. They really like sweet liquids like nectar and honeydew.
- **Where they live:** Native to Argentina, Brazil, Paraguay, and Uruguay. Introduced all over the world.
- **Where they nest:** Argentine ants build shallow underground nests.

Argentine ants are invasive. They have taken over areas that other ants once lived in.

Argentine ants have invaded cities and natural areas all over the world. Wherever they go, they force the native ants out of the area. This is very bad for the plants and animals that need the native ants to help them. Many people don't like Argentine ants because they destroy the natural ecosystem. Argentine ants are also human pests. They spoil food like pastries, sweets, and fruit. These ants also harm crops when they bring aphids into the farmer's fields.

Argentine ant taking nectar from a flower.

Argentine ants form supercolonies that sometimes have hundreds of queens. Workers from different nests recognize each other as family. As you might remember, the largest colony of ants in the world is a colony of Argentine ants.

Argentine ants are native to South America where it floods a lot. They have figured out a way to get away quickly if there is a lot of rain. The ants make nests in leaf litter and the top layer of soil so they can escape quickly when it floods.

Army Ants

Scientific names: *Dorylus, Eciton,* and others

- **Number of species:** Over 200 species.
- **Worker size:** Small to big.
  3/32"-1/2" (3-12 mm).
- **Soldier size:** Big to huge.
  3/8"-9/16" (9-14 mm).
- **Personality:** Aggressive.
- **What they eat:** Army ants eat insects and small animals that are in their way when they travel.
- **Where they live:** Tropical areas from northern Mexico to northern Argentina, Asia, and Africa.
- **Where they nest:** Army ants are **nomadic**. They travel and do not make true nests. They make short-term nests in tree cavities, burrows, and logs when they rest during their travels.

Army ants march through forests eating every insect and small animal in their path.

Army ant colonies have two phases: nomadic and resting. During the resting phase army ants make a temporary nest. Some army ants make a nest by holding onto each other. They make big a ball of ants. In the middle of the ball is the queen. The queen lays eggs all day and all night during the resting phase.

When army ants are done resting, they go into their nomadic phase and start traveling again. They make long, wide trails as they move through the rainforest floor. They look just like an army of marching soldiers. Army ants eat everything in their path, sometimes eating 100,000 insects and small animals in a day!

Army ant workers are all blind. They use smells to communicate and stay together.

Some army ants, like these red driver ants, live mainly underground.

Fire Ants

Scientific names: *Solenopsis*

- **Number of species:** Over 200.
- **Worker size:** Small to medium-sized. 1/16"-1/4" (2-6 mm) long.
- **Personality:** Aggressive.
- **What they eat:** Fire ants have a general diet, but they prefer to **scavenge** for dead animals and insects. They also milk honeydew from aphids.
- **Where they live:** Native to South America. They have invaded North America, Australia, and Asia.
- **Where they nest:** Fire ants build mounds. They usually nest in lawns and grassy areas.

Fire ants have a sting that burns, so be careful around their nests.

There are two species of fire ants that are invasive, the red imported fire ant and the tropical fire ant.

Red imported fire ants are very aggressive. They kill native ants wherever they go. Some scientists think red imported fire ants may have caused other species of ants to go extinct.

Red imported fire ants have a long stinger and strong venom. The sting burns a lot. That's why they are called "fire ants". When their nest is disturbed, red imported fire ants swarm by the hundreds. They run up anything near their nest, clamp onto it, and sting again and again. Many people end up in the hospital after being stung by fire ants.

When an area floods, red imported fire ants make rafts by holding onto each other. The queen and larvae stay safe in the driest part of the ant raft. If there is a drought, fire ants dig deep tunnels until they hit water!

Ghost Ants

Scientific name: *Tapinoma melanocephalum*

- **Worker size:** Tiny.
  1/25"-1/16" (1-2 mm) long.
- **Personality:** Timid.
- **What they eat:** Ghost ants eat many different kinds of food including honeydew and sweet leftovers from people. They also hunt and scavenge for insects.
- **Where they live:** Probably native to Asia. They have spread to many tropical areas of the world, especially in Africa.
- **Where they nest:** Ghost ants nest in soil, rotting logs, bark, flowerpots, and clumps of dry grass.

Ghost ants get their name because of their see-through abdomens and legs. They turn colors depending on what they are eating. If you feed them sugar water with food coloring in it, the ants change colors!

If ghost ants get in your house, they can be really annoying. They love sweet things and invade houses where sweets are left out. If you see tiny ants around a sugar bowl, they are probably ghost ants. In nature ghost ants farm aphids and other insects to get sweet honeydew.

Ghost ants and jumping spiders sometimes live together and help each other. The ants provide a good place for the spider to make its web. The spider protects the ants from predators!

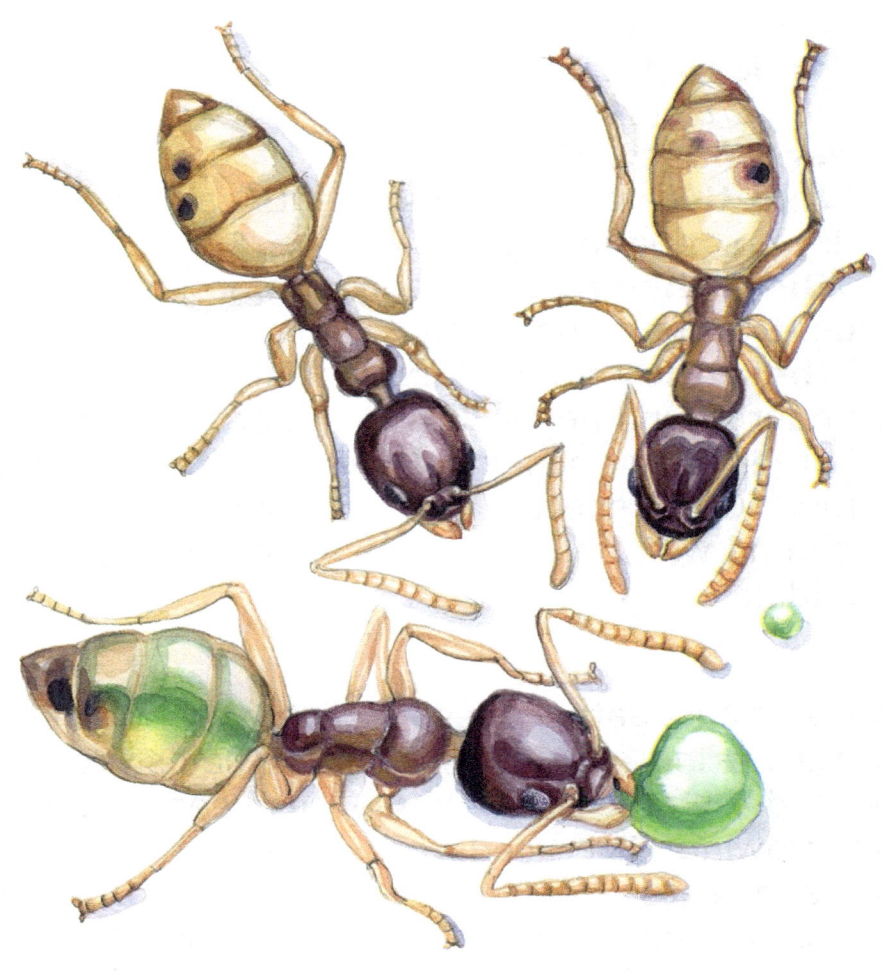

This ghost ant is eating green sugar water.
It makes the ant turn green!

Harvester Ants

Scientific names: *Pogonomyrmex, Messor,* and others

- **Number of species:** More than 160 species.
- **Worker size:** Tiny to big.
  1/16"-3/8" (2-10 mm).
- **Soldier size:** Big to huge.
  3/8"-5/8" (10-15 mm).
- **Personality:** Timid.
- **What they eat:** Harvester ants eat seeds, flowers, and leaves.
- **Where they live:** Savannas, grasslands, and desert areas worldwide.
- **Where they nest:** Harvester ants build deep underground nests. Above the ground, some harvester ant nests look like a maze made of mud. Other species make a mound above the ground with an upside-down cone in the middle.

Harvester ants gather seeds and other parts of plants that they bring back to their nest. They store seeds in very dry storage chambers. This keeps the seeds from growing. The seeds can be stored for a long time and eaten long after they were gathered. Although harvester ants eat mostly seeds, they won't pass up a dead insect or spider if they find one! These animals are also taken back to the nest and eaten.

Fun fact: *A cool fact about harvester ants is that the soldiers have huge heads and strong jaws. Their jaws are so strong that they can break seeds that are hard for people to crush!*

The harvester ants grind up the seeds to make a moist flour called "ant bread". The ant bread is stored in special chambers called granaries, or it is fed to larvae.

A harvester ant carries a seed back to the nest where it will be eaten.

Harvester ants eat lots and lots of seeds.

Hotrod Ants

Scientific name: *Ocymyrmex*

- **Number of species:** About 40 species.
- **Worker size:** Medium-sized.
  1/4" (7 mm) long.
- **Personality:** Timid, but aggressive when disturbed.
- **What they eat:** Hotrod ants eat insects that they hunt or scavenge.
- **Where they live:** Deserts and savannas south of the Sahara Desert in Africa.
- **Where they nest:** Hotrod ants make deep underground nests in sandy soils. Their nests are very well organized. They dig deep underground, and sometimes make tunnels and chambers up 2 yards (2 meters) deep!

Hotrod ants like very hot environments and are often seen running around during the hottest part of the day. That's why they are called "hotrod ants". They have long, thin bodies with long legs and big, muscular heads. They use their long legs to run really fast over the hot sand.

In the hot places hotrod ants live, other insects have to rest because the heat makes them weak. That's when hotrod ants catch these heat-struck insects and take them back to the colony to eat later.

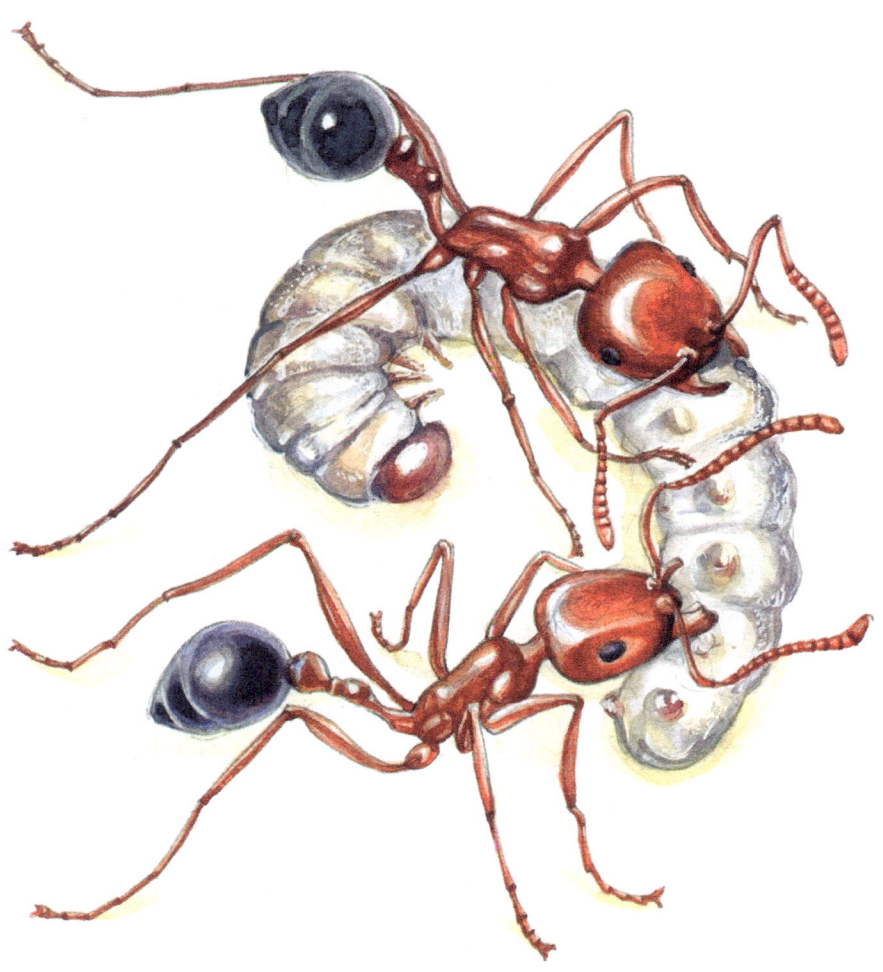

Hotrod ants eat lots and lots of other insects.

Some hotrod ants block the entrance to their underground nest with stones. The bearded hotrod ant gets its name from bristles under its mouth that look like a beard. These hairs are used to pick up sand when cleaning out their tunnels.

Hotrod ants can carry insects much bigger than them. Here a hotrod ant in Africa has found a dead beetle.

Leaf-cutter Ants

Scientific names: *Atta* and *Acromyrmex*

- **Number of species:** Over 47 species.
- **Worker size:** Tiny to huge.
  1/25"-5/8" (1-16 mm).
- **Personality:** Timid, but aggressive when disturbed.
- **What they eat:** Leaf-cutter ants eat sugars made by a fungus.
- **Where they live:** Tropical parts of South America and southern parts of the United States.
- **Where they nest:** Leaf-cutter ants make complex nests deep underground with large round mounds that show above ground. They often nest in grassy patches of the rainforest where the sunlight keeps the area warm.

Leaf-cutter ants are a special kind of ant found in the jungles of South and Central America. These ants make their own underground fungus farms! The leaf-cutter ants cut leaves into pieces and bring them back to their chambers. In the underground chambers, a special fungus grows on the leaves. The fungus grows so fast that there's a lot of extra fungus for the ants to eat.

The fungus and the ants help each other. The ants feed the fungus, clean the fungus, and keep it free of diseases. In exchange, the fungus gives the ants something to eat.

This relationship has evolved for over 30 million years. Now the two species rely on each other so much that the ants can't survive without the fungus, and the fungus can't survive without the ants. When a leaf-cutter queen starts a new colony, she flies away with a small piece of fungus. The queen brings the fungus into her new nest and starts her own fungus-farming colony.

Fun fact: Leaf-cutter ants collect so many leaves from one tree that they could kill the tree. The tree has a way to fight back though. The tree fills its leaves with a toxin that kills the fungus. The ants realize that the leaves from that tree are killing the fungus, so they leave that tree alone.

Leaf-cutter ants gather leaves to feed the fungus in their nest.

Odorous Ants

Scientific name: *Tapinoma sessile*

- **Worker size:** Tiny to small.
  1/25"-3/32" (1-3 mm) long.
- **Personality:** Timid, but aggressive when disturbed
- **What they eat:** Odorous ants love sugar and oily foods that they get from people's houses and the juices of rotting fruit, dead insects, and the insects they farm.
- **Where they live:** North America.
- **Where they nest:** Odorous ants are a common household pest. They nest in electronic equipment, potted plants, cracks in the kitchen, and other strange places. Outside they can be found nesting in soft soils, rotting logs, around garbage cans, and under rocks.

Odorous ants really stink! That's how they got the name "odorous ants". If they are crushed, they smell like blue cheese or paint thinner. The smell is not always unpleasant, but it's strong! When their nest is disturbed, they run out of the ground and spray the air with a smell like rotten coconut.

Similar to Argentine ants, odorous ants form supercolonies. When conditions are perfect and there is lots of food around, they have multiple queens in the same colony. Luckily, they are not an invasive species.

They are sometimes a pest when they invade people's houses. Odorous ants love honeydew and they farm insects that make honeydew. This causes problems when they bring insect pests into orchards and farm fields.

Odorous ant workers take care of the eggs, larvae, and pupae.

Pavement Ants

Scientific name: *Tetramorium*
Featured here: *Tetramorium immigrans*

- **Number of species:** Almost 600 species.
- **Worker size:** Small. 3/32" (3 mm) long.
- **Personality:** Timid, but aggressive when defending the colony.
- **What they eat:** Pavement ants eat dead and live insects, seeds, and honeydew. They also eat human food like meat, grease, nuts, potato chips, cheese, and bread.
- **Where they live:** The United States, Europe, southern South America, and the Mediterranean.
- **Where they nest:** Pavement ants often nest under the pavement, concrete, and rocks.

Pavement ants are very common in the city. Sometimes they become pests when they nest under the foundation of a house. When this happens, they come into the house and look for food.

If you see soft piles of sand or dirt in the cracks of the sidewalk, you are probably looking at the entrance to a pavement ant nest. They get their name because they dig under paved surfaces like sidewalks and driveways.

Pavement ants are usually very friendly. But in late spring or early summer, you can see them having huge battles with neighboring colonies on the sidewalk.

You might also see pavement ants when the queen takes her mating flight in late summer.

Pavement ants are a great species of ant to raise if you decide to have an ant farm. They are fun to watch and easy to care for.

Pavement ants are common in cities. To find their nests, look for a circle of dirt in sidewalk cracks.

Sugar Ants

Scientific name: *Camponotus*

- **Number of species:** Over 1,000 species and subspecies.
- **Worker size:** Medium to big. 1/4"-3/8" (6-10 mm).
- **Soldier size:** Big to huge. 1/2"-9/16" (12-14 mm).
- **Personality:** Gentle, but aggressive when defending the colony.
- **What they eat:** Sugar ants love sweet things like honeydew and nectar. They eat insects and other small, dead animals too.
- **Where they live:** All over the world and found in a wide range of habitats.
- **Where they nest:** Some sugar ants nest in rotten trees, logs, stumps, and dead branches. Other sugar ants make nests underground.

Carpenter ants are one kind of sugar ant. They are one of the most beautiful ants in the world. They are large and often have amazing colors ranging from black to reddish brown. They have large eyes. If you get a close-up view of their heads, you'll see that they look like aliens! Carpenter ant soldiers have very big heads and are large and strong.

Carpenter ants don't destroy the wood of houses. The only nest in wood that is already rotten.

Carpenter ants get their name because they burrow into rotten wood to make their nests. They can't make their nests in solid wood though. So, if you see a carpenter ant nest, you know the wood is already rotten.

Some carpenter ants communicate using sound as well as smells. The workers pound on the wooden sides of their tunnels when their nest is in danger. The sound can be heard by ants up to 8 inches (20 cm) away.

Not all sugar ants are carpenter ants. The hairy sugar ant seen here is found in Africa foraging on flowers.

Thief Ants

Scientific name: *Solenopsis molesta*

- **Worker size:** Tiny. 1/32" (1.4 mm) long.
- **Personality:** Timid, but aggressive when defending the colony.
- **What they eat:** Thief ants like greasy foods, insects, and meat. They sometimes eat sugary food.
- **Where they live:** Tropical areas in the United States.
- **Where they nest:** Thief ants nest almost anywhere. This makes it easy for them to find new places to live. They make their nests in soft soil, rotting wood, under rocks, and cracks in houses.

Thief ants like to nest close to other ants. Besides foraging on their own, they steal food from the nearby colony. Sometimes thief ants live inside the host colony without the other ants even knowing!

Thief ants are beautiful golden ants and have colonies with many workers. If there is enough food in the area, the colony will have many queens.

Because thief ants are so small, they can get into sealed packages of food in people's homes. This makes them an unwelcome house guest. If you have tiny yellow ants in your house, they are probably thief ants.

Thief ants sneak into the nests of other colonies and steal their food!

Fun fact: *Another cool fact about thief ants is that sometimes a new queen will fly off with one or two worker ants attached to her. The workers help the queen start new a colony!*

Trap-jaw Ants

Scientific names: *Odontomachus* and *Anochetu*

- **Number of species:** Over 70
- **Worker size:** Big. 1/2" (13 mm) long.
- **Personality:** Timid, but aggressive when hunting and threatened.
- **What they eat:** Trap-jaw ants are meat-eaters. They hunt many different kinds of insects, spiders, and worms. They also scavenge dead animals.
- **Where they live:** North, Central and South America, Asia, Australia, and Africa.
- **Where they nest:** Trap-jaw ants build nests in soil, leaf litter, cracks in trees, and under bark and rocks. Sometimes they make nests in termite mounds.

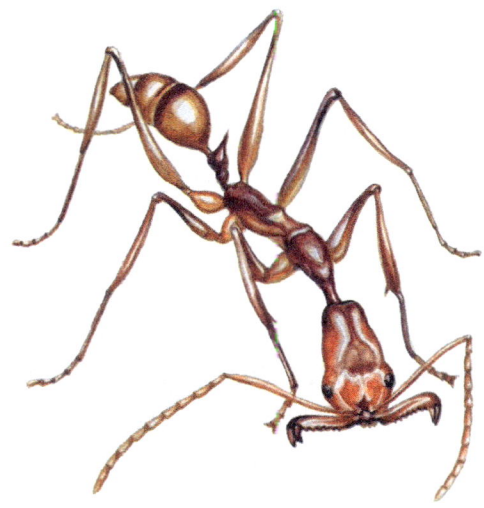

Trap-jaw ants have jaws that snap shut with lightning speed when hairs on the inside of their jaws are touched.

Trap-jaw ants can close their jaws incredibly fast. The only animal on Earth that can close its jaws faster is the Dracula ant! Trap-jaw ants have spring-loaded jaws that close over 2,000 times faster than the blink of an eye. Their long jaws open up to 180 degrees and close around insects at lightning speeds.

Trap-jaw ant with long antennae and strong jaws.

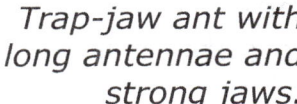

Maybe even more amazing is how trap-jaw ants use their jaws to get away from danger! They point their heads down, snap their jaws shut, and launch off the ground. They can fling themselves over 3 inches (8 cm) high! That is like someone who is 4'5" tall jumping over 33 feet in the air!

Trap-jaw ants have a long, wasp-like stinger that paralyzes other insects. If someone bothers a trap-jaw ant, the ant will sting the person. The sting hurts more than a honey bee sting!

The larvae of trap-jaw ants have sticky pads on their backs. The adults stick the larvae to the ceiling of their nest. This keeps the larvae out of the way.

Weaver Ants

Scientific name: *Oecophylla*

- **Number of species:** 2
- **Worker size:** Small to medium-sized. 3/32"-1/4" (3-6 mm) long.
- **Soldier size:** Big to huge. 5/16"-3/8" (8-10mm).
- **Personality:** Aggressive.
- **What they eat:** Weaver ants mostly hunt insects in the tree canopy and on the ground. They also farm caterpillars for honeydew.
- **Where they live:** Tropical and subtropical parts of Africa, Asia, and Australia.
- **Where they nest:** Weaver ants build their nests in trees. They make nests from leaves connected by silk made by their larvae.

Weaver ants get their name from the cool way they weave leaves together to make their nests. They use silk made by their larvae to join leaves together. Adult ants hold the larvae in their jaws like a tube of glue, and the larvae squirt silk in the space between leaves.

Weaver ants have big eyes and are really good at seeing movement. This helps them hunt insects.

If the tree that weaver ants live in is shaken, the ants fall out of the nest like rain onto the intruder. Thousands of ants swarm and bite the invader, driving it away.

Farmers gather weaver ant nests and put them in their fruit and cocoa trees. The weaver ants kill and eat insect pests that would otherwise harm the trees.

People eat weaver ants in Thailand, India, and other Asian countries. The adults and eggs are made into a spicy chutney. The chutney is not only delicious, it is also considered a superfood.

After larvae squirt silk between the leaves, adult leafcutter ants pull the leaves together to make their nest.

Bonus fun fact: There is a fungus that makes ants into zombies! The fungus takes over an ant's brain and tells the ant to climb a blade of grass. Then part of the fungus grows out of the ant's body and releases **spores**. The spores are like fungus seeds that float down and turn other ants into zombies!

This ant has been turned into a zombie by a fungus that took over its brain! Fungus spores will fall to the ground and turn other ants into zombies!

11. Jobs and Careers with Bugs

Do you enjoy spending time outdoors and learning about nature? Do you love watching bugs? Have you ever wondered what it would be like to work with insects as part of your job?

A person who studies insects for a living is called an **entomologist**. That is just a big word for "bug scientist". If you're an entomologist, you get to work in some really amazing and interesting places.

Insect scientists get to choose which bugs they want to study. So, if you don't like cockroaches, but you think butterflies are cool – no problem! You can study butterflies! With literally millions of bugs in the world, there are lots of insects you can work with.

Insect scientists work with bugs of their choice.

Insect Research

Scientists study the role insects play in nature and the impact insects have on our daily lives. The scientists who do research on insects use their knowledge in many ways. For example, some researchers study insect pests and try to figure out how we can protect our fruit and vegetables from the bugs that damage them.

Many entomologists work in the wilderness. They study insect populations and the effect that things like invasive species, wildfires, and cities have on insects.

Other researchers keep insects in a laboratory at different temperatures to test how they will respond to climate change. The possibilities of study are almost endless. There will always be questions for you to answer if you become an insect scientist!

People who study insects can work outside in nature or in a laboratory.

Helping the Police

Entomologists can help solve crimes too! You already learned that ants help break down the bodies of dead animals. Well, ants are not alone in this job. Insects like flies and beetles help too.

Flies and beetles lay their eggs on the bodies of dead things. When the eggs hatch, the larvae eat whatever has died. Entomologists know exactly how long it takes for the insect eggs to turn into larvae and pupae.

When the police find a human body, they often call a **forensic entomologist**. This is an insect scientist who loves solving crimes! The entomologist looks at the fly and beetle larvae at the crime scene. This tells them exactly when the person died.

The entomologist can also tell if a body was moved after death. If they find insects at the crime scene that don't naturally occur in that area, it is possible that the bugs were brought there with the body.

Insects and Education

Zookeepers take care of butterfly houses and ant farms at the zoo. People go there to watch insects go about their daily lives. Visitors to the zoo see how insects help us and how they interact with the world around them. People also see the importance of insects in their gardens and other natural areas.

Some museums have insect collections with insects from all over the world! These collections are put together by **curators** at the museum. The collections allow people to see insects that they might never have known existed.

You can see there are many exciting jobs if you love insects. Someday you can have one of these cool jobs!

Curators at museums have huge insect collections they show to visitors.

12. A Note from The Folks at Wild Pages Publishing

Dear Reader,

Thank you very much for reading our book about Ants!

We get great feedback from parents, teachers, and children who have enjoyed this book. We hope you liked it too!

If you did, please leave a 5 Star review on Amazon. Your review really helps out a lot. :-)

In fact, your 5 Star review is probably the most appreciated thing you can do for us! There is a link or QR code for you below.

This Ants book is the first book in the Nature Discovery Books for Children Series. We are excited to write this series for you and your loved ones.

At Wild Pages Publishing we are committed to helping kids solve the mysteries they find in nature. Our goal is to help children learn and discover about planet Earth and the plants and animals here.

Our staff includes people who have deep connections with nature. We are biologists, teachers, educators, best-selling authors, and scientists... and some of us have lived off-grid.

We all grew up with a strong fascination for wild places... forests, deserts, lakes, and streams. Each of us are excited to pass on our learning, love, and respect for nature to children all over the world. We hope you and your children are inspired to discover more about our amazing world!

Again, if you and your children have enjoyed this book, we'd like to ask you to leave a great review on Amazon. We love knowing that we've given something to you and your family. And, reviews help others discover our books.

Please leave a nice review for us by typing https://www.bklnk.com/review/B0BS8ZZWK7 into your web browser. Or you can point your phone camera at the QR code below and tap the link that appears below the QR code on your phone.

Thank you so much!

The Folks at Wild Pages Publishing

QR Code for leaving a review on Amazon

13. Glossary

Adapted from the Britannica Kid's Dictionary (2022) (https://kids.britannica.com/kids/browse/ dictionary), unless stated otherwise.

Abdomen: The hind part of the insect body behind the thorax (chest).

Adapted: Changed in a way to fit a new situation and a specific purpose.

Antennae: A pair of thin, movable sensing organs on the heads of insects. One of these is called an antenna.

Ants: Small insects that are related to bees and wasps and live in colonies where different individuals do special duties.

Aphids: Small, soft-bodied insects that suck the juices of plants.

Atmosphere: The layer of gas or "air" that surrounds the earth.

Chambers: Rooms in a house, often referring to bedrooms.

Colonies: A population of plants or animals living in a particular place and belonging to the same species.

Curators: People who build and care for collections in museums and zoos.

Decomposition: The breakdown or rotting of plant or animal matter.

Eco-friendly: Not harmful to the environment (from Cambridge Dictionary).

Ecosystem: A natural system made up of a community of living things interacting with their environment, especially under natural conditions.

Environment: The world around us, including everything that can influence the ability of living things and communities to survive in their surroundings, for example: the climate, soil type, different plants and animals, food availability, and shelter.

Entomologist: A person who specializes in the study of insects.

Female: A girl, woman or a female plant or animal. The gender that can have babies or lay eggs (not all female ants can lay eggs, only the queen lays eggs).

Forensic entomologist: A scientist who studies the process of insects decomposing a dead body for the purpose of a criminal investigation (from Wikipedia).

Fungus: Living things like molds, mushrooms and mildews that grow on dead or decaying organic matter like tree stumps or in other moist environments like bathrooms. More than one of these are called fungi.

Habitat: The place or type of place where a plant or animal naturally or normally lives or grows.

Honeydew: A sugary liquid made by aphids or scale insects.

Humidity: The amount of water or moisture present in the air.

Insects: Small animals without an internal skeleton, where the body is clearly divided into a head, thorax, and abdomen, with six legs and usually one or two pairs of wings.

Invasive: A living thing not native to a particular area that causes economic or environmental harm when it moves into the new area (paraphrase from National Geographic).

Larvae: Young, wingless and often worm-like forms of insects (like grubs or caterpillars) that hatch from eggs. One of these is called a larva.

Life cycle: The series of life stages, body forms and activities through which a living thing passes from its own birth to the birth of its children or offspring.

Male: A boy, man or a male plant or animal.

Native: Living or growing naturally in a particular area.

Nectar: A sweet liquid given off by plants, especially by the flowers, that is used by bees in making honey.

Niche: A habitat or place that has all the things necessary for a particular plant or animal to live.

Nomadic: People or animals with no fixed home, who wander from place to place. They are called nomads.

Pheromones: A chemical substance like a scent or smell that an animal makes to communicate with other individuals of the same species.

Pollen: Tiny particles in the male parts of a flower that fertilize the seeds and usually appear as fine yellow dust.

Predators: An animal that obtains food mostly by killing and eating other animals (called the prey).

Prey: An animal that is hunted, killed and eaten by another animal (called the predator).

Pupae: Insects in the developmental stage between being larvae and becoming adults, usually enclosed in a cocoon. One of these is called a pupa.

Queen: The fertile female of social insects such as bees, ants, and termites whose main purpose is to lay eggs.

Scavenge: To feed on dead animals.

Society: A system or group of living things that depend on each other and usually form a social unit, such as human beings or a hive of bees.

Species: A group of living things of the same kind, made up of related individuals able to reproduce and have fertile offspring.

Spores: The reproductive cells of fungi, some plants, ferns, and bacteria). Usually one cell and can produce a new individual from the spore.

Thorax: The middle of the three main parts of the body of an insect.

Worker ants: The female members of a colony of social ants that perform most of the labor and protect the colony.

Zookeepers: The people who keep or care for animals in a zoo.

Start your Own Ant Farm!

If you would like our free Guide to Getting Started with an Ant Farm and to get our new books for free, please go to **https://wildpagespublishing.com/antfarmoptin**

Wild Pages Publishing's Guide to Getting Started with an Ant Farm

Nature Activities for Children Book Coming soon...

Be on the lookout for more books from Wild Pages Publishing.

We are excited to bring you a whole series of plant, animal, and natural science books.

And...

In the works is a book of Nature Activities for children! This book will have fun, educational outdoor activities for children of all ages.

We can't wait to share it with you!

Made in the USA
Monee, IL
09 August 2025

22946343R00046